And Others

The Bible and the Child

And Others

The Bible and the Child

ISBN/EAN: 9783337172909

Printed in Europe, USA, Canada, Australia, Japan

Cover: Foto ©ninafisch / pixelio.de

More available books at **www.hansebooks.com**

The Bible and the Child

The Bible and the Child

By

The Very Rev. F. W. Farrar, Dean of Canterbury
The Rev. Robert F. Horton
Arthur S. Peake, M.A.
Professor Walter F. Adeney
The Very Rev. W. H. Fremantle, Dean of Ripon
The Rev. Washington Gladden
The Rev. Frank C. Porter
And the Rev. Lyman Abbott

New York
The Macmillan Company
London: Macmillan & Co., Ltd.
1896

Norwood Press
J. S. Cushing & Co. — Berwick & Smith
Norwood Mass. U.S.A.

Contents

I

The Higher Criticism and the Teaching of the Young 1

    By the Very Rev. F. W. Farrar, D.D., Dean of Canterbury.

II

The Higher Criticism and the Teaching of the Young 29

    By the Rev. Robert F. Horton, D.D.

III

The Higher Criticism and the Teaching of the Young 51

    By Arthur S. Peake, M.A., Tutor in Biblical Subjects, Primitive Methodist Theological Institute, Manchester, England.

IV

The Higher Criticism and the Teaching of the Young 69

> By Professor Walter F. Adeney, M.A., Professor of New Testament Exegesis, History, and Criticism at New College.

V

The Higher Criticism and the Teaching of the Young 89

> By the Very Rev. W. H. Fremantle, D.D., Dean of Ripon.

VI

The Bible as Literature 109

> By the Rev. Washington Gladden, D.D.

VII

The Higher Criticism and the Teaching of the Young 127

> By the Rev. Frank C. Porter, Ph.D., Professor in Yale Divinity School.

Contents

VIII

The Bible as Rearranged by Modern Criticism . 151

By the Rev. Lyman Abbott, D.D., Pastor of Plymouth Church, Brooklyn.

I

The Higher Criticism and the Teaching of the Young

By the Very Rev. F. W. Farrar, D.D.
Dean of Canterbury

The Bible and the Child

I

I AM asked to say a few words upon a subject of real and urgent importance — "the right way of presenting the Bible to the young in the light of the Higher Criticism." I gladly accede to the request, because an unwise or unfaithful way of dealing with the facts forced upon us by the advance of knowledge may be prolific of deplorable results.

The change of view respecting the Bible which has marked the advancing knowledge and more earnest studies of this generation is only the culmination of the discovery that there were different documents in the Book of Genesis — a discovery first published by the physician Jean Astruc, in 1753. There are *three* widely divergent ways of dealing with these results of deep research, each of which is almost equally dangerous to the faith of the rising generation.

1. Parents and teachers may go on inculcating dogmas about the Bible and methods of dealing with it which have long become impossible to those who have really tried to follow the manifold discoveries of modern inquiry with perfectly open and unbiassed minds. There are a certain number of persons who, when their minds have become stereotyped in foregone conclusions, are simply *incapable* of grasping new truths. They become obstructives, and not infrequently bigoted and furious obstructives. As convinced as the Pope of their own personal infallibility, their attitude towards those who

see that the old views are no longer tenable is an attitude of anger and alarm. This is the usual temper of the *odium theologicum.* It would, if it could, grasp the thumbscrew and the rack of mediæval inquisitors, and would, in the last resource, hand over all opponents to the scaffold or the stake. Those whose intellects have thus been petrified by custom and advancing years are of all others the most hopeless to deal with. They have made themselves incapable of fair and rational examination of the truths which they impugn. They think that they can, by mere assertion, overthrow results arrived at by the lifelong research of the ablest scholars, while they have not given a day's serious or impartial study to them. They fancy that even the ignorant, if only they be what is called " orthodox," are justified in frantic denunciation of men more truthful and incomparably more able than themselves. Off-hand dogmatists of this stamp, who usually abound among professional religionists, think that they can refute any number of scholars, however profound and however pious, if only they shout " Infidel!" with sufficient violence. But, as the holy Bishop Ken says :

The *older* error is, it is the worse;
Continuation may provoke a curse.
If the Dark Age obscured our fathers' sight,
Must, then, some shut their eyes against the Light?

If there were no opposition to critical inquiry, except what is of this crude kind, it would hardly be deserving of any notice, but might be passed over with silent disdain. There are, however, many true and tender souls, incapable of severe studies, and wedded to beliefs which they have identified

Very Rev. F. W. Farrar, D.D.

with their holiest hours, who are too old or too fixed in opinion to make progress, and who, from honest dread lest they should be dragged into doubt respecting views dear to them as life, cannot get rid of the belief that there is something "wicked" in free inquiry. Like Cardinal Newman, they think it their duty to treat their reason as though it were a dangerous wild beast to be beaten back with a bar of iron. Ought they not to bear in mind the warning of the great Bishop Butler that our reason is the *only* faculty we possess by which we can judge of *anything*, even of Revelation *itself?*

Besides this large class of Christian people, there are always some who, with the same temper of mind, but with more ability and knowledge, are ready to supply masses of tortuous "harmony" and casuistically plausible conjecture, which may give a semblable possibility to the old views. The impossible and dreary nature of the defence serves to deepen in other minds the conviction that the cause which needs *such* arguments is lost. I can only say, in my own case, that when, more than forty years ago, I came to the conclusion that the Book of Daniel, as we now have it, could not have seen the light before the age of the Maccabees, my conclusion was indefinitely strengthened by reading Dr. Pusey's treatise in defence of its genuineness and authenticity.

We cannot greatly respect the possibly pious but obstinate and illiterate priest who, having been accustomed to read the impossible word "*mumpsimus*" to his congregation, on being corrected indignantly grumbled that he was not going to give up "his old '*mumpsimus*' for their new '*sumpsimus*.'" But every one should be a little ashamed and

Very Rev. F. W. Farrar, D.D.

afraid to be of those who are the last to give up their adherence to opinions which have long become naturally obsolete. "There is nothing so revolutionary," said Dr. Arnold, "because there is nothing so unnatural and convulsive, as the strain to keep things fixed, when all the world is, by the very law of its creation, in eternal progress, and the course of all the evils in the world may be traced to that natural but most deadly error of human indolence and corruption, that it is our duty to preserve and not to improve." A study of the past shows us that it has been one of the chief duties of each age in succession to cast off the slough of old ignorance. The advance of knowledge is a direct work of God's revealing power. "God shows all things in the slow light of their ripening;" and since the light of all certain knowledge which comes to us from the long results of time is light from heaven, how can it lead us astray?

This, at any rate, is certain, that if children are still taught to regard as articles of their religious belief opinions about the inerrancy, universal equal sacredness, verbal dictation, or supernatural infallibility of *all* that is contained between the covers of the sixty-six books which we call the Bible, the faith of those children, if they develop any intelligent capacity or openness of mind hereafter, is destined to undergo a rude and wholly needless shock, in which it will be fortunate if much of their religion does not go by the board. Some of those Books of Scripture are separated from others by the interspace of a thousand years. They represent the fragmentary survival of Hebrew literature. They stand on very different levels of value, and even of morality. Read

Very Rev. F. W. Farrar, D.D.

for centuries in an otiose, perfunctory, slavish, and superstitious manner, they have often been so egregiously misunderstood that many entire systems of interpretation — which were believed in for generations, and which fill countless folios now consigned to a happy oblivion — are clearly proved to have been utterly baseless and egregiously false. Colossal usurpations, of deadly import to the human race, have been built, like inverted pyramids, on the narrow apex of a single misinterpreted text. From the days of Origen (A.D. 253) to those of Nicholas of Syra (A.D. 1340) the whole science of exegesis was stultified by non-natural attempts to read into all Scripture a fourfold sense (literal, allegorical, mystical, spiritual), much of which was as absurd as the Jewish Cabbala.

The old forms of allegorical interpretation which, from the days of Philo to those of

The Bible and the Child

Bishop Wordsworth, once crowded enormous commentaries with useless irrelevance, would be simply laughed at if they were offered to us in these days as though they possessed any validity.

> For I see that through the ages one increasing purpose runs,
> And the thoughts of men are widened by the process of the suns.

Of all ways of dealing with "the Higher Criticism," none is more futile, and none will more certainly bring its own Nemesis, than that which thinks it sufficient to brand its followers with charges of wilful faithlessness, and to crush them with impotent anathemas, which will only rebound upon the heads of those who utter them.

2. Another way, equally common among ignorant and incompetent controversialists

Very Rev. F. W. Farrar, D.D.

of the opposite extreme, is to talk as if the Higher Criticism had robbed the Bible of all value, and had shown it to be a mass of falsity and imposture. Here again it requires some knowledge of language, of literature, of history, of national idiosyncrasies, to be even capable of estimating the real nature of a result arrived at. Ignorant and irreverent attempts to discredit and vilify the Bible are even more egregiously illiterate than the idle super-exaltation which would turn it into a fetish or an amulet.

Let me give an instance or two.

The immense majority of scholars of name and acknowledged competence in England and Europe have now been led to form an irresistible conclusion that the Book of Daniel was not written, and could not have been written, in its present form by the prophet Daniel, B.C. 534, but that it can have been

The Bible and the Child

written only, as we now have it, in the days of Antiochus Epiphanes, about B.C. 164, and that the object of the pious and patriotic author was to inspirit his desponding countrymen by splendid specimens of that lofty moral fiction which was always common among the Jews after the Exile, and was known as "the Haggadah." So clearly is this proven to most critics that they willingly suffer the attempted refutation of their views, which are often very insolent as well as very futile, to sink to the ground under the weight of their own inadequacy. Even Delitzsch, a truly learned man, and "orthodox" by every instinct of his mind, after vainly trying to hold out against modern conclusions, found the love of truth too strong within him to admit of his continuing to resist arguments to which he felt that he could furnish no valid answer. Those who understand the

Very Rev. F. W. Farrar, D.D.

Bible aright find the intelligent faith cleared and strengthened by better knowledge of the books which they reverence; but some ignorant sceptic gets hold of this conclusion about the age of the Book of Daniel, and declares to gaping audiences that scholars and divines regard the book as no longer sacred, but as an unblushing fable and an impudent forgery. He does not tell his ill-educated hearers that among those who find the critical conclusion so irrefragable as not to require any further argument have been found some of the ablest and most instructive commentators on the book, and that only by reading it in the light of its true date is it possible for us fully to grasp the bearing of its moral and spiritual lessons. Still less does he see that when he talks of "falsity" and "forgery" he is using idle misjudgments and anachronisms, which only reveal his own incompetence to understand the correct significance of literary problems. He is judging the methods and views of the second century before Christ by the literary standards and habits of the nineteenth century after Christ.

Or let us take the case of the Pentateuch. Those who now regard it as a matter of demonstration that, in its present form, it embodies the handiwork of at least four different writers, and that it contains at least three varying strata of legislation, do not, on that account, lose one essential element of its moral greatness and religious teaching. One case may illustrate this. In the Book of Leviticus[1] a large space is occupied by the arrangements and ceremonies of the Day of Atonement, and the way of dealing with the scapegoats, and now it is known to all stu-

[1] Lev. xv.

Very Rev. F. W. Farrar, D.D.

dents that, except in the Book of Leviticus, there is not so much as the dimmest trace of any observance of the Day of Atonement, not even in passages where, by every law of literature and psychology, we should have thought it most certain that such allusions would be found — not even, for instance, in the account of Hezekiah's or Josiah's Reformations, not even in the elaborate Levitism of the Book of Ezekiel,[1] not even in the reorganization of Judaism in the days of Ezra and Nehemiah. It is said that this is a mere *argumentum e silentio;* and they must indeed be easily convinced who accept that phrase as an adequate reply. Is it, then, nothing that what would not naturally have been regarded as a *central* ordinance of religion, and as the unique day of the religious

[1] 1 Kings viii. 27 seq.; Ezek. xiv. 18–20; Zech. vii. viii.; Ezra iii. 1, 6; Neh. viii. 13–17.

year, should not so much as once be alluded to in the entire religious literature of the nation, and that the *first* allusion to the only instituted fast-day in the Jewish year should be in an Apocryphal Book — Ecclesiasticus — in the third or second century before Christ? It is, to me, almost humiliating to see on what slight straws of a mere phrase many will be content to rest the weight of great conclusions. Would any one be able to persuade us that the festivals of Christmas and Easter had been from the early days among the most sacred of Christian festivals, if not a trace of them, not an allusion to them, were to be found in a thousand years of Christian literature? On this ground, then, *alone*, is it not inevitable that many should be led to doubt whether the Day of Atonement can be proved to have been originally of Mosaic origin? And how much

Very Rev. F. W. Farrar, D.D.

more if that inference is strengthened by many quite different, yet converging, lines of argument, all tending to the same conclusion? But, supposing that we are unable to resist this inference, in what single respect does it weaken our sense of the deep and blessed symbolism enshrined in the ordinances of that unique day in the Jewish year? Is one moral or spiritual lesson about the exceeding sinfulness of transgression, and the mercy of God, and the gracious revelation of God's forgiveness of sins to the sincerely penitent, in any way weakened or dimmed by holding that the institution of the scapegoats and the blood of sprinkling originated at a later rather than at an earlier date? Is the light of revelation granted to mankind only in intermittent flashes at intervals of millenniums? Or, rather, is the Spirit of Man the candle of the Lord, and is there

The Bible and the Child

a Light that lighteth every man that is born into the world?

3. There is a third way of treating the Higher Criticism — even more common than either of the other ways, less unwise, perhaps, but still undesirable. It is simply to ignore all critical results. This, however, is not so easy, and at the best it is but the ostrich policy which tries to bury its head in the sand in order to escape its pursuers. Modern discoveries are already beginning to be recognized in books written for the use of the young which are indispensable to the Biblical teacher. If children are left unaware that the views of those most competent to represent their generation are widely different from those which were all but universal in the days of their grandfathers, the discovery will certainly come to them later on, and may come so suddenly as to imperil their

Very Rev. F. W. Farrar, D.D.

faith. If overgrowths of alien ivy are suffered to become too dense and vigorous, and to thrust their fibres into the interstices of every stone, then, when it is necessary to tear them away, it is often found that they have seriously injured the stability of the building which they were originally intended to adorn; have too long been suffered to injure and enshroud. If we would save the building from destruction and decay, we must cut away the ivy directly we begin to perceive how injurious may be its effects.

If, then, the methods (1) of denunciation, (2) of exaggerated misapplication, and (3) of silent ignoring be unwise, what *should* be the attitude of parents and teachers to the Higher Criticism? It has always been my humble endeavour to speak without any subterfuge and with perfect plainness, and though space forbids me from developing the subject here,

The Bible and the Child

I hope that the following brief remarks and aphorisms may be found serviceable by the thoughtful and the sincere.

I. We should be profoundly and unswervingly *truthful*. We ought never to practise that *falsitas dispersatura*, that "economy of truth," which found favour among some of the Fathers, and has often been an avowed principle of action in the Church of Rome. Truth is too sacred a thing to admit of manipulations or juggling. Traditionalism, or professionalism, or self-interest should never for a moment be suffered to obscure our sense of its eternal obligation. We are not bound to teach children all we know, but we are most solemnly bound not to teach them anything which we feel to be doubtful as though it were certain, and still more are we bound not to teach them anything of which we ourselves begin to suspect the reality.

Very Rev. F. W. Farrar, D.D.

II. Into a vast part of our teaching, by far the largest and most important part of it, no question of the Higher Criticism enters at all. The object of the best and most sacred Bible teaching is to form the character, not to store the intellect. It is moral; it is spiritual; it has to do with things eternal; it far transcends all minor questions of the date or historicity of the books in which it is enshrined. Does a child fail to grasp the meaning of the parables of Christ though he is told that these are not necessarily founded on real incidents, but are "tales with a purpose"? Why, then, should it be different with the stories, say, of Balaam or of Jonah? There is a remarkable book by Dr. H. Oort, written in Dutch by a pupil of the great Professor Kuenen and under his supervision, called *The Bible for the Young*. It has been translated into English, and goes much further, on many points, than I should myself go; but it is a learned and most interesting book, and it demonstrates that there need be no evaporation of one of the best lessons of Scripture even in the hands of teachers who are advanced votaries of the Higher Criticism. Not even the most timid need make a bugbear of recent results. They become harmful to the cause of "sound learning and religious education" only when they are glaringly misused by their adherents or by their antagonists.

III. The manner in which the Higher Criticism has slowly and surely made its victorious progress, in spite of the most determined and exacerbated opposition, is a strong argument in its favour. It is exactly analogous to the way in which the truths of astronomy and of geology have triumphed over universal opposition. They were once

Very Rev. F. W. Farrar, D.D.

anathematized as "infidel"; they are now accepted as axiomatic. I cannot name a single student or professor of any eminence in Great Britain who does not accept, with more or less modification, the main conclusions of the German school of critics. In Germany itself, the land of laborious and devoted study, there are scores of learned professors, and among their entire number there is said to be only one — and he a man of no name — who clings to the old "*mumpsimus.*" Truth is great, and will prevail.

IV. Our knowledge of Scripture will not remain stationary now any more than it has done in the past. On the contrary, there never was an age in which we were more likely to be led to new truths of interpretation than this. For in this age the increase of all sources of information has been unprecedented, and we can now read the Bible in the light of a philology, a literary breadth, an acquaintance with comparative religion, and an insight into history and psychology, such as have never been equalled in any past century. We are not using the language of boastful arrogance, but of profound gratitude to Him who is the Light, the Truth, and the Way, when we say of this generation,

> We are heirs of all the ages, in the foremost files of Time.

We should do well, then, to take to heart the wise warnings of four great and holy theologians who lived before the Higher Criticism was even dreamed of — Hooker, Bishop Butler, Richard Baxter, and J. Robinson.

" Whatsoever is spoken of God, or things appertaining to God," says Richard Hooker, " otherwise than truth, though it seems an honour yet it is an injury. And as incredi-

Very Rev. F. W. Farrar, D.D.

ble praises given unto man do often abate and impair the credit of their deserved commendation, so we must likewise *take great heed lest, in attributing to Scripture more than it can have, the incredibility of that do cause even those things which it hath most abundantly to be less reverently esteemed.*"

"And here," says the great and good Richard Baxter, "I must tell you a great and needful truth, *which Christians, fearing to confess, by overdoing, tempt men into infidelity. The Scripture is like a man's body, where some parts are but for the preservation of the rest, and may be maimed without death.*"

"I am convinced," said the pastor John Robinson, in his farewell address to the Pilgrim Fathers before they sailed in the *Mayflower* from Delft Harbour, "that the Lord hath yet more light and truth to break forth from His Holy Word."

The Bible and the Child

And Bishop Butler thought it "not at all incredible that a book which has so long been in the possession of mankind should contain many truths as yet undiscovered."

V. To conclude, then, no one who fearlessly loves and follows the truth will have the smallest difficulty in co-ordinating the teachings of Scripture — and all the more in proportion as he wisely loves the Bible — to the results of modern inquiry. He will still be able to say with the large-minded Quaker poet of America:

> We search the world for truth; we cull
> The good, the pure, the beautiful;
> From graven stone and written scroll,
> From all old flower-fields of the soul.
>
> And, weary seekers of the best,
> We come back laden from our quest,
> To find that *all the sages said*
> *Is in the Book our mothers read.*

II

The Higher Criticism and the Teaching of the Young

By the Rev. R. F. Horton, D.D.

II

To some of us it is a matter of amazement that the misunderstandings — I will not venture to say the misrepresentations — connected with this subject should be so persistent and obstinate. It taxes all our charity to find men, good men, presumably religious men, continuing to discuss the question in a spirit of blind and uninquiring prejudice. They will not take the trouble to learn what it is, about which they so confidently affirm. With a scorn which is the twin-sister of ignorance, they seek to stamp out truth by humiliating and deriding its advocates. Were ever the genuine advocates of truth so intemperate, so denunciatory, so blind, and so ignorant as the men who have been loudest in the outcry against the Higher Criticism? The only parallel in history is the tone of the Pope — the infallible Pope — and even the Pope is nowadays more courteous. I hope it is not a severe judgment, but I believe this tone of anger and vehement anathema is only found, and can be only found, when men are defending positions which in their hearts they suspect to be insecure. When the foundations are suspected, the defenders will use any device to prevent an examination of them. If you propose to rest your religion on an infallibility of any sort, the only chance is to surround your infallibility itself with an inviolable ring which forbids criticism, and to resent any suggestion of doubt, dealing with it as impiety to be denounced, and not as argument to be met. Now, what is the issue in this long and excited controversy? It is

The Rev. R. F. Horton, D.D.

simply this: Are we required to accept the Bible—just as it stands—as the voice of God in such a sense that to question any of its assertions is blasphemy, or to examine the composition of its books is an offence against the Holy Spirit who wrote it? Or, on the other hand, are we permitted and even required to study the books, and find out all we can about them, in just the same way that we deal with other literature, and then allow the voice of God to speak to us as it will through the books thus studied and understood?

The old orthodoxy, which these angry critics still accept, decided the question in the first way. The Bible from Genesis to Revelation was a smooth, consistent voice of God, like a Delphic Oracle. One was to read it as God's letter to the human race. If you came across any contradictions or inconsistencies, you were to attribute these to your own feebleness of apprehension, but never allow that there could be anything wrong in the book. Piety was to be proved by showing that the inconsistencies were harmonized. If, for example, it said in 2 Chron. xvii. 6 that Jehoshaphat " took away the high places and the Asherim out of Judah," and then in Ch. xx. 33, " howbeit the high places were not taken away," it was a proof of reverence to the infallible word to show how the high places were both taken away and not taken away by Jehoshaphat because "the Word of God" cannot be broken. If in reading the Bible you came across sentiments of fierce retaliation or deeds of savage bloodthirstiness, against which a man of ordinary morality might naturally revolt, it was your duty to justify these sentiments because they were the Word of God, and to find excuses for

The Rev. R. F. Horton, D.D.

the deeds because they were recorded without censure in the Word of God. You were not allowed to argue that because the sentiment was not godly it could not come from God, or because the deed was unchristian it could not be approved by God. That was treated as presumption, as judging God, as setting up the intellect against its Maker.

This was and is the decision of the old orthodoxy. And what is its result? Plymouth Brethrenism on the one hand, and infidelity on the other. It is this view of the Bible which has enabled the infidel publication, *Reynolds' Newspaper*, to regale its Sunday readers lately with columns of extracts from the Bible which run counter to even a worldly man's sense of righteousness, as the "Word of God." If the Plymouth Brethren account of the Bible is correct, *Reynolds' Newspaper* is justified. As to the honesty of Reynolds in

The Bible and the Child

assuming that Plymouth Brethrenism is the religion of Christendom, and ignoring that no man of scholarship or education holds the view of the Bible which would justify this procedure, I will say nothing, for that is a side issue. But while the loudest and most vehement defenders of the Bible persist in advocating this impossible view, infidelity will have a thousand weapons ready to its hand.

Now I venture on the assertion that the result of criticism has been to take all these weapons out of the hand of every honest sceptic. When Reynolds, or any other infidel teacher, bases his attack against the Bible and Christianity on this unintelligent view of the Bible, he convicts himself of ignorance. He starts from premises which no one grants — I mean no one but Plymouth Brethren and the small number of Christians

The Rev. R. F. Horton, D.D.

who have set themselves against the fair examination of the Bible. The simple fact is that this old view of the Bible is not justified by any assertion of the Bible itself, unless some misquoted and misapplied texts, which even ignorance hesitates to cite, are to carry the day; texts just as much misquoted, misapplied, as those which are supposed to support the Papacy; nor is that old view supported by any external authority of Church or Council, or even unbroken tradition. It is not consistent with the use which the New Testament writers made of the Old; and it goes to pieces, like a mummy brought into the fresh air, directly any unbiassed mind begins to study and examine the Bible to see exactly what it is.

Now, of course, I am not contending that the critics are right in their conclusions; all I say is that they are justified in their methods. Not only are we allowed, we are literally required, before the Bible can give its real message to the world, to bring every resource of scholarship, the examination and collation of manuscripts, the emendation of the text, the consideration of authorship and style, the internal evidences of dates, the witness of archæology and history, and above all the developed system of Christian life and teaching, to settle the exact bearing, relation, and authority of each book and each section of the Bible. Unless and until this is done, the Bible may be wrested by selected citation, by ignorant confusion of dates, and purposes, and application, or by an arbitrary method of allegorizing, to teach just what each man wishes it to teach. And in place of the Divine Truth, which must be one and absolute, you have every man his own exegete, and every exegete his own Pope; and

The Rev. R. F. Horton, D.D.

presently, as the system develops, you have the world rising up impatiently against these myriads of petty Popes, as it did once before against the imposing, though effete, single Pope. The answer to Popery is not that private judgment which makes every one an authority entitled to speak *ex cathedrâ* from the Bible, but that free, honest, and reverent study of the Scriptures, aided by all the best scholarship of the age, which tends more and more to make Biblical Theology an intelligible and progressive system, and in its highest Christian development a final test and authority in religion.

It is no answer to the critical method to prove that Wellhausen has made mistakes — the critical method is not bound up with the infallibility of Wellhausen — or that Cheyne is arbitrary in fixing the dates of the Psalms. The only real refutation of it would be to furnish some proof from the Bible, or from God, that we are forbidden to make these candid inquiries into the structure of the literature; or, if you will, to show that the Christian religion is injured instead of being cleared and strengthened by the fearless use of those faculties which God has given us. for the discovery of truth. Neither of these has been done. Indeed, I will venture to close with an illustration, which is one of a thousand easily adducible, to show how *religion* gains, if orthodoxy suffers by the candid work of criticism.

Let us turn to the 137th Psalm. I suppose no one was ever so far blinded by tradition as to think that David was its author. It tells its own tale. It was written five centuries after David's time, by an exile in Babylon. But according to the traditional orthodoxy, this exile psalmist was the pen-

The Rev. R. F. Horton, D.D.

man of the Holy Ghost. He uttered the sentiments which God breathed into his heart, and told him to commit to writing. Any of these verses might therefore be quoted as *the Word of God.* That was the theory. And consequently it must be regarded as a beatitude pronounced by God on any man who should take the little innocent Babylonian children and dash them against the rock. It is not a sentiment that seems suitable in the heart of the Father of our Lord Jesus Christ; and the old orthodoxy must bear its own responsibility for maintaining a dogma which made such a conclusion inevitable. But there was a greater difficulty still. The Lord had spoken through Jeremiah, xxix. 7, commanding the exiles to seek the peace of Babylon, and to pray to Him for it. How could the same God have breathed into the exile psalmist this cruel and bloodthirsty sentiment?

I need not labour the point to prove how religion gains, how the truth of God gains, how Christ's view of God is established, by a mode of handling the Bible which emphatically denies that this bitter thought of the exile was God's thought at all, a mode of handling the Bible which, instead of treating every passage in the Bible as the Word of God, seeks diligently to find and understand the Word of God, which is unquestionably there.

The Higher Criticism, we may depend on it, is of God, and whatever is to be said of individual scholars, the *method* must prevail, to the lasting benefit of religion, of the Church, and of mankind.

When it is once realized that the result of criticism has been, and will be still more,

The Rev. R. F. Horton, D.D.

not to lessen but to intensify the spiritual value and the teaching power of the Bible, it will be the plain duty of both parents and Sunday-school teachers to start in the instruction of their children from the position which criticism has securely established. The baseless dogma about the nature of the Bible must not be given to the children; the Bible itself must be given. But more. Not only must the Bible itself be given, but it must be given with so clear and convincing an explanation of what the Bible actually is, that children may escape the "sunless gulfs of doubt" into which we and our fathers were plunged.

I mentioned Psalm cxxxvii. as an instance of the spiritual illumination and the clearing of the ethical teaching, which may be gained by fearlessly applying criticism to Scripture. I was very much affected by the words of a

The Bible and the Child

dear old friend, a faithful and loving Christian from his boyhood, who told me how a difficulty of many years' standing had been removed by my exposition of this Psalm. How could it be otherwise? What miserable confusion must be wrought in the mind of a child if he is taught that the awful imprecation—

> Happy shall he be that taketh and dasheth thy little ones against the rock.

is the Word of God! It is impossible, in the face of such an error, to give children a true idea of the God and Father of our Lord Jesus Christ.

Nor can I forget the storms of unbelief to which I was subjected as a boy in preparing the Book of Judges for a Cambridge Local Examination.

No pastor or master ever hinted to me that the deeds of treachery or blood in that

The Rev. R. F. Horton, D.D.

book, wrought by men on whom the Spirit of God was said to have come, were not approved by God Himself. I supposed that the dastardly deed of Jael was religiously praiseworthy, and that Samson must be a character that we should do well to copy.

I know, of course, that a large proportion of the boys brought up with me on the same principles of Biblical interpretation have actually become unbelievers — or, at least, callously indifferent to the Bible. A few like myself have been saved from that melancholy fate by the revealing light and truth which, under the hand of diligent critics, " have broken forth from the Word " in the last twenty years.

And if I may be pardoned another personal reminiscence, the first shock to faith which I received in Oxford was not from the so-called unbelief, or from the philosophical speculations, of the University, but from preparing the Book of Acts for the entrance examination. It was in a shady room, looking out on the loveliness of the New College gardens, that I was confronted by the fact that the speech of Gamaliel referred to certain predatory outbreaks which did not occur until *after* the date of his speech. If I had encountered such an error in Thucydides or Livy, it would not have shaken my confidence in those great historians; but to meet with a historical slip in an Infallible Book shook the whole untenable foundation of my faith. I speak, therefore, from my own experience of sorrowful and unnecessary shocks to the religious life when I plead that a true view of what the Bible is should be placed before children from the beginning.

The Rev. R. F. Horton, D.D.

I think I must also mention an incidental injury which a wrong conception of the Bible has wrought in the training of the young. The unreality and tedium of much Sunday-school teaching, which issue in the children leaving early and imbibing a permanent dislike to the Christian Church, must have an explanation. It is easy to lay the blame at the door of the teachers. It is inadmissible to charge the fault on the Bible itself. Surely the mistake lies in the conception of the Bible which most teachers are themselves taught, and feel in their turn bound to teach. They have to smooth over and explain away the moral incongruities or the historical discrepancies of Old Testament scriptures. They have to give an allegorizing meaning to passages which in the original intention could have had no such meaning. For instance, a worthy cor-

The Bible and the Child

respondent assured me, some years ago, that Esther was to him the most precious of books, because after much prayer it had been revealed to him that Ahasuerus is Almighty God, Mordecai our Lord Jesus Christ, and Haman the Devil. My correspondent is the editor of a widely read newspaper and represents the orthodox ideas of Bible interpretation. But to teach children a view of that kind is fatal. It not only must destroy all respect for the Bible; but also, what an idea of God must it give them if they are to see Him in the arbitrary and sensual Persian king, or what an idea of our Lord if they are to interpret Him by the hard and cruel character of that bitterhearted Jew! As for Haman, I am ready to admit that he may present a plausible portrait of the Devil; but it would leave on the child's mind the impression that the

The Rev. R. F. Horton, D.D.

Devil has been hanged, which is unfortunately not true.

May I conclude by commending to Sunday-school teachers two admirable pamphlets written by Charles Edward Walch, of Hobart, Tasmania; one on Sunday-school teaching, the other on Gospel sickness. The second of these is published by James Clarke and Co. They are full of sense and religion; they show how an earnest Sunday-school teacher had himself discovered the need of Biblical criticism before he had become acquainted with its work; and they suggest that a new day of vital interest in the Sunday-school and in the home teaching of children will begin when the true view of the Bible has become generally known and accepted.

Meanwhile, every child should be taught from the first that the Bible is a compilation of many different books, written by different authors and at widely distant periods of time. He should be taught that these books constitute a rough record of the stages by which God has been revealed to the world, and of the difficulties, the doubts, the rebellions, which His gradual self-revelation has encountered among men. No word should be said about the Bible being infallible, for the term is wholly misleading. And every effort should be made to show that *Christ is the end of the law*, so that the teaching should rather be what Christ is, has done, and is doing in the world to-day than the slow and dubious steps by which the world was prepared for His coming. The latter is a necessary study for theologians. The former alone is needed for, and is capable of, riveting the attention of our little children.

III

The Higher Criticism and the Teaching of the Young

By Arthur S. Peake, M.A.

Tutor in Biblical Subjects, Primitive Methodist Theological Institute, Manchester

III

AMONG the awkward questions that the Church has to face we must set that of the best methods to be chosen in bringing before our young people the results of Biblical criticism. To some it is not awkward at all, either because they are unaware of the attainment of such results or because they roundly refuse to believe in them. Others will not entertain it, on the too popular principle, "Why can't you let it alone?" Those of us who are satisfied that real results have been won, and that for the advancement of the faith it is vital that they should not be kept back from our young people, cannot acquiesce in a conspiracy of silence. However awkward, the

The Bible and the Child

question is most pressing, and on the way it is answered much of the future depends. There is not even this excuse for silence, that if we say nothing they will hear nothing. The truth is quite otherwise. They will hear much that is crude and garbled, but roughly effective none the less, and if they hear it all unprepared, their position is dangerous indeed. They have learnt no defence, and believe that Christianity is hit in a vital place. How much better if they already know, and know better than those who flaunt these things in their face, what the results of criticism really are, and know, too, that their feet are planted on a rock of certainty which no criticism can shake. If I may repeat a phrase I used in an article some years ago, criticism "has drawn the fangs of the secularist lecturer"; perhaps I ought to add: only he is not aware of it.

Arthur S. Peake, M.A.

In other words, criticism has swept away many of the things most chosen by the Secularists for attack. It is our privilege to place our young people at the right point of view, and preserve a faith which shall not be incompatible with intellectual integrity. We must vaccinate them with criticism to save them from the small-pox of scepticism.

When we pass to the methods to be employed, it will be readily seen that the question is largely one of presuppositions. We find a set of ideas about the Bible already in possession when we begin our work. Children in Christian homes form their views of the Bible from the reverence always paid to it, its use in family worship and in the Church, and all the other indications that it is to be regarded as a book quite sacred and apart. Why it should be

The Bible and the Child

so treated they hardly know; it is taken for granted as part of the natural order of things. They know nothing of Inspiration. I remember when I was eight years old reading some of *The Antiquities* of Josephus. I was very much interested, and said, "Why, this is just like the Bible." I was told that Josephus was not inspired. What with the child is unreasoning acceptance becomes with the boy or girl intelligent acceptance, but on grounds received without question. In this state of mind good and bad elements mingle, and the good probably predominate. It is highly important that the Bible should be reverenced as the record of the revelation and redeeming activity of God, that it should be set above all other books, and indeed placed in a unique position. But it is not well that this should be held to involve extravagant claims for the Bible —

Arthur S. Peake, M.A.

claims beyond what it makes for itself or beyond what can be established by sound proof. Yet these are almost universal, and constitute the great difficulty of the teacher.

The first thing to be done, if our young people are to be taught the critical view of the Scriptures, is to destroy their illusions. And this will be done by various lines of proof. I scarcely venture to suggest what order should be followed, but I will name some of the points it is necessary to prove. The corruption of the text both of the Old and New Testaments must be urged to prove that Providence has not attached so much importance to the exact transcription of the words of the autographs as to secure miraculous immunity from errors of copyists. This may be used with great force against the doctrine of verbal inspiration, and it should be shown that in many cases the best scholars are not agreed as to the true reading. Another thing that should be insisted on is that there is no orthodox doctrine of Inspiration, in other words, there is no doctrine to which the Church is committed. This may be shown by pointing to the great variety of view that has prevailed on the subject, and, therefore, since the question is not closed, we must claim, as Protestants, the right of private judgment upon it. In this connection it is well to adduce the example of the leaders of the Reformation, Luther and Calvin, who treated the Bible with considerable freedom. Next it might be shown that the popular view of the Bible has largely come to us from the rigid scholastic theologians of the seventeenth century, whose conclusions in some other departments of theology we are almost unanimous in rejecting. It might then be pointed out that they came to their doctrine of Scripture in an *a priori* way, and formed it with very little reference to facts. The essential irreverence of this method should be brought out in that it presumed to form a theory of what God must have done, instead of humbly setting to work to discover what He had actually done. Over against this false method, which has given us the popular view, the true scientific and historical method should be set. The teacher should make it clear that the only satisfactory way is not to spin theories out of one's own inner consciousness, but to set to work patiently to investigate the phenomena which the Bible presents, and form the doctrine as a result of the investigation. It might be well to enforce this by instances, from other departments of knowledge, of the ignominious end of passionately defended *a priori* theories. Another illusion, which is persistent and troublesome, is what is known as the "all or nothing" doctrine. It springs directly from the popular view that the Bible is a whole, of equal authority and of equal inspiration from end to end. If a single error is admitted, the Bible cannot be inspired at all. This is often very difficult to deal with, and the teacher cannot be too careful in his treatment of it. Once this has been cleared away, the path will be comparatively easy. The proof of the falsity of this position should come from several sides. The most important thing is to show that for the purpose for which it is assumed that the Bible was given, such errors in matters of fact as are alleged are unimportant. The moral and religious value remains unimpaired. This might be illustrated by those numerous passages in

Arthur S. Peake, M.A.

both Old and New Testaments which speak to us with such an immediate and authentic Divine voice, that they carry with themselves proof of their own inspiration. In this way the impression of inspiration does not depend on perfect historical accuracy, as to which we could never from the nature of things be sure of our ground, but on the conviction that the voice of God alone could say such things to us. The testimony is that of our own religious consciousness. In this way the belief in inspiration will be placed on a firmer basis, while it will be detached from such an accretion as a belief in inerrancy. The "all or nothing" argument may be met in another way by pointing out the unfairness with which it treats the Bible. If a man discovers a blunder in his daily paper, he does not jump to the conclusion I have heard formulated with reference to

The Bible and the Child

the Bible in this way: "If all of it ain't true, there's none of it true." A man should treat his Bible as fairly as he treats his newspaper. It is unfair in another way. We have no right to expect of the Bible more than it professes to give. And it makes no claims to inerrancy. On another side an effective appeal may be made to Christian loyalty. We cannot place the words of any one on the same level as the words of Christ. This helps us to recognize distinction of value in various parts of the Bible, and the argument may be reinforced by illustrations of the fact that some portions of the Bible speak much more directly to our souls than others. It is also of great importance to emphasize the fact that the Bible is not a book, but a collection of books, gradually formed, and fluctuating in extent so that even now Protestant scholars cannot regard

Arthur S. Peake, M.A.

the limits that should be set to the Canon as fixed beyond dispute. These may serve as hints of the way in which this difficulty should be met.

The removal of illusions is only one, though the most important, part of the preliminary work. It should be supplemented by the positive proof that the position taken up is better in itself. These are some points that should be made clear. Criticism has made the Bible more precious to us because it has made it intelligible and interesting. It has made the uniqueness of the religion of Israel and of Christianity stand out with far greater clearness. It has driven us to Christ, the only "impregnable rock," as our supreme religious authority. It has thus withdrawn apologetics from the useless task of defending shattered outworks to the invincible fortress itself. And if it be urged that the authority of Christ guarantees the traditional authorship of Old Testament books, it must be said in reply that the Incarnation involved a surrender of omniscience that He might be like us in all things except sin, and that even if His knowledge on these points transcended that of His own time, it would have been to cast a needless stumbling-block in the way of His hearers to discuss critical questions with them. The relation in which the Son stands to the universe did not cause Christ to reveal the secrets of nature, which our own age has so largely discovered, nor to correct the astronomical errors of His contemporaries.

One point more may be briefly mentioned. It is of great moment that while the teacher is conducting his class over this delicate ground he should make abundantly evident his own devotion to Christ and the Gospel.

Arthur S. Peake, M.A.

The practical problem that presents itself to the pupils is: If I revise my views of the Bible, how do I know that I shall not end by giving up Christianity? Nothing will reassure him more than the feeling that the teacher is a living example of the reconciliation of faith with criticism.

So much for the preliminaries. It is so much, because they are the most important. Who should the teacher be? In most cases, I think, the minister — that is, where he has been sufficiently conscientious to give earnest study to the subject. I have further assumed that a class will be formed for the systematic study of the subject. Such a course as I have already sketched will take some time, and then the actual teaching of the subject will begin, and will need continuous work. As a rule, critical questions should be let alone in the pulpit. They may unsettle the faith of older Christians who are unable to distinguish between form and substance; and, apart from this, the pulpit is meant for another purpose. The class might consist of any who wished to join, but I think it would be prudent to admit none under fourteen, and perhaps that limit is too low. A text-book is badly wanted, and till a satisfactory one appears each teacher must make his own. Professor Robertson's *The Old Testament and its Contents* might be used at a pinch, but those who are not satisfied with a halfway house will prefer to wait for something more critical. The question of the New Testament is less pressing. Dr. Dods' *Introduction to the New Testament* or Mr. M'Clymont's *The New Testament and its Writers*, would do as a text-book. Common sense will indicate the necessity of placing only those results before a class, which are

Arthur S. Peake, M.A.

generally accepted by critics. As to the order, I should suggest that the Hexateuch be taken first, since here the work has been most completely and perhaps most finally done. If I were writing for students who wished to examine the subject for themselves, I should recommend a different order, but this will, I think, be found best in this case. There is no need to sketch an outline of study; a teacher who knows his subject will find the line that suits him best. But, on another point, is it too much to ask of the officials and Church that if they cannot help they will at least not hinder the work? They cannot be more anxious for the welfare of the young people than the minister. And in his efforts to keep them, by making Christianity credible to them, they may rest assured that he will not play fast and loose with the essential truths of the religion in which, in common with themselves, he finds his highest inspiration and joy. The wisest policy is to trust him and let him take his own course. We are in a time of change, and the only thing which will preserve the unity of the Church is the love that " hopeth all things " and " believeth all things," even the orthodoxy of the minister who is a critic.

IV

The Higher Criticism and the Teaching of the Young

By Walter F. Adeney, M.A.

Professor of New Testament Exegesis, History, and Criticism at New College.

IV

I HAVE no doubt that to many readers the suggestion that the Higher Criticism should be brought into any connection with the teaching of children must seem about as absurd as a proposal that Quain's *Anatomy* should be made up into reading-lessons for an infant class. The very association of the phrases is almost as incongruous as, say, the pairing of a whale with a violet. It should be remembered, however, that when we refer to the teaching of children we are not always thinking of the A B C lessons of lisping babes. There is more difference in mental grasp between a child of four years and a boy or girl of fourteen than there is between the latter and a man or woman of forty. Even young children have an awkward habit of springing upon us, in the most unconscious innocence, questions which persons who are acquainted with the results of the latest research can only answer honestly in the light of that research. This is the point. It is not to be supposed that any sensible people are eager to transform the rising generation into an army of critics. The judgment is the latest faculty to ripen; with some of us it seems to remain green for a lifetime. To urge the exercise of it prematurely is only to rear an ugly crop of prigs.

What, then, have children to do with the Higher Criticism? I should say that their relation to it is concerned with the results rather than with the processes. Let us clearly understand what we mean by this often repeated phrase, "the Higher Criticism." The angry style in which it is handled by the more ignorant of those people who take upon themselves to heap indiscriminate denunciation upon it, would seem to imply that it was simply an indication of the self-conceit of its authors, who meant by the use of it that their critical methods were superior to the methods of less advanced students. A more ridiculous misinterpretation can hardly be imagined. Of course, as every student of its first elements knows, the Higher Criticism is not so named as being better than an inferior criticism that it affects to despise, but simply in contrast with another kind of criticism, which is equally valid in its sphere — the lower criticism concerning minute questions of the settlement of the original text, etc., and the higher passing on to inquire into the age, authorship, character, and ten-

The Bible and the Child

dency of the books it concerns, as far as these can be ascertained from an examination of their contents. Surely no reasonable person can object to such a study being pursued, although it is quite open to any competent person to say that it is erroneously carried on by some of its disciples. One thing, I think, may now be affirmed in regard to this matter. There are whole reaches of inquiry that have been so thoroughly surveyed that we can no longer treat them as lying in the mists of uncertainty. The fog has lifted over these regions, so that we can see their outlines. In other cases, where perhaps we were once accustomed to think we could discern the capes and bays of a sharply marked coast-line, the powerful telescope of criticism may prove that we were only gazing at a bank of clouds. That cannot but be an unsatisfying result to arrive at; and yet our personal disappointment is no excuse for smashing the telescope. At all events, it is best to know the facts. Then the question arises, If we know the facts, what reason or justification have we for continuing to teach children just as we did before we had reached them? I have no wish to perplex and puzzle children with abstruse questions; but I feel the grave mistake of ignoring the fairly established results of criticism. We may not be able to explain Kepler's laws to young children, but that is no excuse for doggedly persisting in representing to them that sun, moon, and stars all revolve round the earth.

One of the commonest mistakes about the Higher Criticism is that it only issues in a mass of dreary negations. I am by no means ready to take a brief for every person

The Bible and the Child

who chooses to style himself a critic. There are men who come to the consideration of Biblical problems with a marked prejudice against the transcendental, the spiritual, everything that is not in agreement with everyday London club life — men who are so obviously blind to the religious wonder of revelation that they put themselves out of court at once when they set forth their arid negations. Their criticism is as uncritical as Jeffreys's criticism of Wordsworth. By every word they utter they prove themselves to be inhabitants of another world from that of the inspired writers, and therefore utterly unfit to present themselves as their judges. There are men, too, with whose character and temper we may have no reason to quarrel, and yet who are manifestly so extravagant and one-sided that what they give out as critical results must

Walter F. Adeney, M.A.

only be accepted by us as *obiter dicta*. But when a full discount has been allowed for all these eccentricities and irrelevances, there remains a heavy balance to the credit of sound criticism, the accumulated returns of the labour of a number of sober workmen whose converging harmony of opinion cannot be brushed aside without impertinence. Now here it is that we find results that are by no means all negative. The mining is not all for the shaking of ancient foundations; the best of it is carried on in new fields for the discovery of hidden treasure, and with the result that already we have been presented with some precious nuggets of gold.

Is it nothing that this criticism has quickened our interest in the Bible — that it has given new life especially to the Old Testament? Some of us who would still fain believe we are young men, can yet recollect the time when there was a manifest danger of the Old Testament falling altogether into neglect among the more progressive teachers of Christian truth. In the present day the study of the Old Testament has come to be courted with the keenest interest. Criticism has thrown new light upon the history of Israel. Formerly the writings of the Hebrew prophets were handled as though they were so many scattered Sibylline leaves. Now they are made to discourse eloquently of the ages from which they sprang, and to reclothe their authors with the flesh and blood of real life. There is no reason why children should not have their share in these happy gains so far as they are able to appreciate them. Then as we pass on to the New Testament we have still larger and richer results of sound criticism. The critical comparison of the Synoptic Gospels one with another and with St. John's Gospel has led to such a clear understanding of the life and teachings of Jesus Christ as was probably never before reached in the history of Christendom. Until quite lately it was customary to mix up sayings of our Lord with texts from any of the epistles, not to mention Old Testament quotations, as though they all ran on the same plane, to the confusion of any character and specific meaning. Now we are able to see the teaching of Jesus in its own crystalline clearness. That is an infinite gain. It is much, too, that the latest criticism has demonstrated the essential unity of that teaching as it appears in all the four Gospels. At the same time, we are able to detect the different standpoints of the several evangelists, and, when we come to the apostles, to see their several ways of presenting the Gospel, each characteristic, each valuable. The truth itself is better apprehended when seen in these various lights than it was when all differences were blurred by the artificial contrivances of the harmonists. Thus the New Testament lives to us with a crispness of outline and a vividness of colour which it owes to the clarifying processes of criticism. Is there any reason why children should not be introduced to these fresh and interesting results?

But now if criticism has yielded us these profits, it cannot be denied that it has unsettled some old-established positions, and here we come to the crux of the matter. The first question will be, How are we to deal with the narratives of the earliest times in the light of criticism? To be simply silent about them is to take the feeblest course imaginable. Though it may not be desirable to set them as formal Sunday-school lessons, just as if they were on a level with the Gospel story, to throw them aside altogether would be to follow a counsel of despair. To put the matter on the lowest ground, a person who has grown up in ignorance of such time-honoured narratives must be held to be uneducated. Moreover, the beauty, the charm, the moral and religious significance of many of these stories will win the hearts of children in the future as they have won the hearts of children in the past. This winsome grace of the antique stories is one of the proofs that they are presented to us with the power and life of Divine inspiration. We cannot afford to lose sight of them, say what the critics may about them. The child's Bible would be sadly impoverished if these favourite parts were to be missing. But let the stories be given in their quaint old-world simplicity. When we are dealing with those concerning which we may think historical grounds of assurance cannot be made out, it will be misleading to drag in allusions to modern geographical and archæological data. The stories should be set by themselves, framed in their own mystery. As soon as the children are able to understand it, they should be informed quite simply, and without any painful sense of reserve, that they are different from the later history, because the books in which they are recorded were not written till many hundreds of years after the times to which they refer. Children soon have to learn how all history begins among the mists of uncertainty, in the dim ages of a far-off antiquity. They know this with regard to the story of Britain, and it does not make them sceptics of the history of the Norman and Tudor lines. If they are told that possibly King Arthur was a myth, they are not thereupon so confused as to doubt the landing of William the Conqueror. These points of difference would be above the comprehension of very little children; I am not now referring to such, but to boys and girls of some growth in intelligence. Take, for instance, the story of Adam and Eve. To know nothing of this would argue gross ignorance; and it is better to come upon it in the grand simplicity of its original form in Genesis than to meet with it for the first time clothed in Milton's strange mingling of Puritan theology and sensuous poetry. This story is not only touched with antique charm; it is replete with profound lessons concerning man, his sin, and his fate — lessons which, coming to us as we receive them in the austere simplicity of the primitive narrative, awe us with a sense of the Divine.

The Bible and the Child

Yet I suppose very few educated people take this narrative as prosaic history. Then why should children not be told that it is an old tale teaching great lessons, and not an account of the way things actually happened?

The case of the patriarchs is not of the same kind. I must confess that I am old-fashioned enough to cling to the stories of Abraham, Isaac, and Jacob; and certainly we have had gleams of light from the desert and the monuments that suggest points of verification. Still, it cannot be denied that the rearrangement of the Pentateuch has raised questions in many minds as to grounds of certitude concerning these narratives. Similarly, the new order in which the records of the Pentateuch are now arranged cannot but affect the whole story of the tabernacle in the wilderness. The plain statement about these things is that the narratives in their

Walter F. Adeney, M.A.

present form were written so many hundreds of years after the events occurred that we cannot be as certain about them as we are about contemporary records. I do not see any reason why we should not say this to children who are old enough to understand what is, after all, a very simple statement. It will be objected that this is a dangerous position, but I venture to affirm that a furtive and timorous reserve is a far more dangerous one.

If, however, criticism touches the New Testament, it is natural to inquire with more anxiety as to what are its effects. Here we have come out into broad daylight, and the answer can be given with more assurance of finality. But here, too, criticism brings us nothing to fear. The effect of the most searching and ruthless inquiry is that the central Figure of all history and all religion stands out with a new clearness of outline,

The Bible and the Child

and at the same time with a commanding majesty, nay, with the awfulness of true Divinity, so that we are constrained to exclaim with Thomas, " My Lord and my God." After that what do the details matter? Yet these details are useful in filling up the background of the canvas. Now it is not so much the Higher Criticism as a mere ordinary literary criticism that has brought to light certain small inconsistencies in the several Gospel narratives. These are puzzling to the historian, whose business it is to settle every disputed point in the story, but they are of no religious importance whatever. The dangerous thing is to attempt to smother them up under a confusion of words. The simple, natural, straightforward course is to admit them without perturbation; for it is not the inconsistency in the narrative but the perturbation in the teacher that upsets the child's faith. If children were not brought up with an unfounded belief in the verbal inerrancy of the Bible, these discrepancies would run off them as water from a duck's back, admittedly real, but incapable of penetrating to the deep regions where faith lives and where doubt may be bred. I was almost saying that those people who so deliberately set the terrible stumbling-block of verbal inerrancy in the path of Christ's little ones are themselves in danger of the millstone; but I know they are acting from the best motives as the friends of the children. Still, what a huge blunder they have fallen into, and how disastrous are its consequences! They believe themselves to be defenders of the faith; but their feverish anxiety seems to be engendered by the unwholesome effluvia of a decaying creed. Faith can look the whole world in the face and welcome light from every quarter, knowing that the foundation standeth sure. When we feel the Spirit of God breathing on us from the pages of the Bible, we may regard the work of criticism with equanimity, having the satisfying inward assurance that no arguments can touch our one supreme, indubitable fact. Without this perception it matters not what becomes of the battle of the critics; at best it can but issue in one more literary verdict with which to cumber the libraries of the learned. Above all, if we have a settled faith in Christ, confirmed by the experience of the Christian life, we might as well imagine that some new theory was about to filch the sun from our sky as fear that any criticism could ever rob us of our Lord. If this is the right position to take up, surely it is our business to lead children into it by the straightest course possible.

V

The Higher Criticism and the Teaching of the Young

By the Very Rev. W. H. Fremantle
Dean of Ripon

V

THE Higher Criticism is often supposed to mean negative criticism, but it really means the criticism, not of texts, but of the underlying ideas of a work. It is, therefore, much more congenial to the faithful and Christian teacher than the Lower Criticism, which deals with manuscripts and readings. Of the works of Lachmann or Tischendorf, or of Westcott and Hort, on the text of the New Testament, only a few scholars can judge; but of the questions raised by Ewald or Kuenen we can all judge. Could the Book of Deuteronomy, they ask, which assumes that there is only one altar, and vehemently condemns worship in the High Places, have been in existence when Samuel, the chosen leader and inspired prophet, sacrificed at the High Place in Ramah; or could the words, "Who saith of Cyrus, Thou art my shepherd, saying to Jerusalem, Thou shalt be built, and to the Temple, Thy foundation shall be laid," have been written by Isaiah one hundred and fifty years before the Temple was destroyed, and two hundred before Cyrus reigned? Of such questions, I say, we can all of us judge. And, further, we are all of us unconsciously among the "higher critics" when, for instance, we read Psalm cxxxvii., and ask whether the words, "Happy shall he be that taketh and dasheth thy little ones against the stones," express the mind of the Divine Spirit, or whether they belong to a class of ideas and feelings which have been done away in Christ. Here Christian faith is itself the Higher Criticism.

Such questions are sure to be asked as the

child grows into the man or woman, and it is of the utmost importance that we should so teach the Bible that they may not prove a fatal stumbling-block. The late M. Taine, one of the foremost writers and thinkers in France, became a Protestant because he felt sure that if his children were taught the literalisms which, in the hands of French priests, made the Bible a tissue of incredibilities, they would, as they grew up, cast away their religion, whereas the sane explanations of the excellent pastors Bersier and Hollard, to whom he intrusted them, would make possible a continuance of belief. We may well ask ourselves whether the cause of the alienation from Christian faith is not often this, that we have bound up with religion during childhood a number of ideas which the adult finds to be untenable, but from which he finds it impossible to disentangle it.

This danger may be to a great extent obviated by showing that what is paramount in the Scriptures, as explained by criticism, is the religious interest. Take the question of the books of the law, on which so much criticism has been expended. The higher critics have mostly come to the conclusion that Exodus, Deuteronomy, and Leviticus contain successive handlings of the law, the rudiments of which came from Moses, just as the Psalms have their source in David, but they believe that each re-editing of the law has a distinctly religious purpose. On this, therefore, the teacher should fix the child's attention. He should show how stress was laid in each epoch upon the points most needful for the religious life: first, in Exodus, for the primitive social life of the nation; next, in Deuteronomy, for the final struggle against idolatry in the period from

Very Rev. W. H. Fremantle

Hezekiah to Josiah; and, lastly, in Leviticus, for the time after the captivity, when the sense of sin and the need of sacrifice were so fully developed. It is not necessary to go into minute criticism with the young; but it is a distinct gain to the teacher, say in reading Deuteronomy, to be able to describe the "hill-altars" and the "Asherim" existing in every corner of Judæa, and the degradation of the worship of God as described by Hosea and the early prophets, and thence to show the need of the limitation of sacrificial worship to the central sanctuary at Jerusalem. And, similarly, it is a gain to realize the state of mind of the Jews in the great revulsion from idolatry under Ezekiel and the second Isaiah, and to associate the lamentations for national apostasy which we find in Nehemiah ix., or Psalms cvi., or the denunciations of Leviticus xxvi., with the passionate longing for atonement with God which brought into prominence the priestly code of Leviticus.

The Psalms and the prophets and histories are comparatively easy to deal with in the light of criticism. In the histories the chief difficulties are caused by various traditions which have been placed side by side, as in the varying accounts of the elevation of Saul to the kingdom, and of David's introduction to Saul. When these are frankly admitted, as they would be in any other case, the difficulty is gone, but the religious lesson is unimpaired. As to the Psalms, the dates and construction of them are still *sub judice;* but this is of little concern for their religious bearing. They are of all ages, and give voice to the universal needs of the human soul. The criticisms, however, of Cheyne, which show that they have a national as well as an individual bearing, should be of use to us in training the young to public and social duty, which is among the greatest needs of our time. As to the prophets, criticism has made them stand out as vivid, struggling personalities, their words gaining force from the clearer disclosure of the special circumstances of their time. How much more real does such an utterance as that of Isaiah lxiv. 10, 11, become—"Zion is a wilderness, Jerusalem a desolation; our holy and our beautiful house, where our fathers praised thee, is burned with fire"—when we think of it as springing warm from the heart of the great unknown prophet of the exile as he depicted with patriotic sorrow the actual state of desolation, than when we try to conceive of it as written two hundred years before, in the time of Hezekiah, when the Temple stood firm and Jerusalem was unscathed by fire.

Let us now pass to a different sphere, that

of the narratives which have created most controversy. Take the account of the Creation. If we believe it to be a poetic vision of the upgrowth of the world under the hand of God, we can surely make the pupil understand this. To be sure, children are, as Goethe said, "inveterate realists," and are sure to ask, "Was it all true?" But the great religious lessons—the universe a great unity, the manifestation of one principle, one agent, and that the Holy One; the world prepared for man, who is to master it and use it according to God's will; the spiritual element supreme over the material, the consecration of the whole by its issue in a Sabbath of holy rest; man made after God's image, his innocence as the witness that sin is not a necessary part of his nature, the sanctification of human love and family and social life by the blessing on the first parents of the race—all this is so preponderant, and in the hands of an earnest teacher can be made to stand out so clearly, that the mere process of creation falls naturally into a subordinate place.

This may rightly lead us to consider the attitude which we should take towards the miracles of the Old Testament. We should dwell on the Divine purpose and its result, not upon the particular mode of working. The word "miracle," as used in Scripture (put Paley aside), is quite undefined, and simply implies to the religious mind a wonderful and striking fact which makes us realize the presence of God. On the action of God, therefore, we should fix the attention. Take the account of the deliverance of Israel by the passage of the Red Sea. We may take the old precritical view which made even Matthew Arnold speak of the narrative as instinct with supernaturalism, or we may, with the *Speaker's Commentary*, take it as wholly natural. The latter is surely the most vivid and attractive; we see, and make the pupil see, the sea driven back by the strong east wind, the storm-cloud helping the Israelites by its lightnings, but beating in the faces of their enemies, the sun as the eye of God looking forth in the morning watch from the pillar of cloud, and the tide returning in its strength. Yet upon none of these in themselves must the attention be fixed, but upon the combination of all these forces under the hand of God for the deliverance of Israel. We need not be anxious to explain the processes through which God wrought, either as identical with or as differing from the processes known to human experience. What we want to impress is the sense of God working out His righteous and

Very Rev. W. H. Fremantle

loving purpose, whether in ways within or in ways beyond our comprehension. And, further, we want to make the pupil realize that the wonder of old time is the heightened or concentrated example of that which is in its essence repeated day by day in the action of God towards us. Even now, with all our advance in knowledge, how little do we know of the secret forces of nature! The saying of Newton is still true, that we are like children picking up shells on the shore of an ocean whose depths are unexplored. Our philosophers have to speak of an "energy" which is the source of all action, yet is in its essence unknown. We may, therefore, with entire frankness, adopt in our teaching such words as those of the Psalmist: "Thy way is in the sea, and Thy paths in the great waters, and Thy footsteps are not known."

There are, we must admit, some stories in the Bible which we cannot take literally, such as that of the axe-head swimming at the word of Elisha, or the three children in the fiery furnace. But a tactful teacher will know how to get over the difficulty. In some cases he will pass it by, as the Germans say, "with light foot," especially where, as in the first of these instances, no spiritual lesson is directly connected with it. In other cases, as in the second of these instances, he may rightly say that, the story being told after three hundred years, it is quite possible that its details have been altered, but that in any case it represents an instance, such as has often been known, of faithful confessors delivered from a cruel death; and he may thus suggest what is the real religious use of the story to us — that God's people are constantly passing through the "smoking furnace" (Gen. xv. 17; compare Deut. iv. 20, 1 Kings viii. 51), and are like the bush bathed in fire, which has suggested the motto of the persecuted Church, "*Et tamin non consumebatur.*"

A similar mode of treatment may be adopted as to the moral difficulties of the Old Testament; they must in some cases be avoided, in some cases explained. But here we are on firmer ground, having the plain declarations of our Lord himself to guide us. He admits the doctrine of development in moral matters. What was "said to the men of old times" needed to be corrected by what He said. Moses gave laws for the hardness of men's hearts which He repealed. The disciples were not to imitate Elijah in calling down fire from heaven. We need not scruple, therefore, to tell our children, as they are able to bear it, that expressions like the long curses of Psalm cix., ending with "Let this be the reward of mine adversaries from the Lord," could not be allowed in the mouths of Christians. With the younger children such passages may best be left unread, and in devotional exercises they must not be introduced. I presume that few pastors who have free choice would dwell upon them in the congregation; and I think that when these passages are set down to be read in the appointed order in church, the liberty which the law now gives to vary the Psalms under special circumstances may be held to justify the exclusion of expressions of hatred. Our congregations contain persons of all classes and all ages, and we must beware of suggesting to young or old what will be certainly perplexing, and may lead to deadly error.

It is in the teaching of the Old Testa-

Very Rev. W. H. Fremantle

ment that the difficulties chiefly arise which it is the design of these papers to meet. But there are difficulties also in the New Testament; and though these are not so numerous, they are aggravated by the fact that the critical results are far less clear. The time at which the Gospels were composed, the account to be given of the wide variations and the minute agreements of the first three Gospels, and of their relation to one another and to the fourth Gospel, are as yet undetermined. On the other hand, many of the discrepancies which have perplexed pious souls, and which have been met by strange evasions or attempts at reconciliation, become non-existent to us as soon as we put aside the fictitious assumption of an exact accuracy in the narratives. We can then say : It matters nothing whether Christ healed two blind men going out of Jericho, as St. Matthew reports, or one blind man coming into Jericho, as St. Luke states; or which of the versions of the title upon the cross, which is given differently by each evangelist, is the true one. We hardly ask such questions in the case of other books, but are content to say: " These are different versions, slightly varied, of the same transaction." There is no difficulty in saying the same as to the Gospel accounts, either to ourselves or to our children. What is more difficult is to make them understand the state of human nature which existed in Palestine in our Lord's time and long after — a state in which leprosy and hysterical affections and demoniacal possession were common phenomena, and in which, therefore, the presence of a Divine personality must produce effects to which our later Western life presents hardly any analogy.

Very Rev. W. H. Fremantle

But something of this kind must be suggested in order to prevent in later years a sense of unreality besetting the subject and obscuring the character and teaching of Christ.

In conclusion, I think that our own religious experience on these subjects is our best guide in teaching. If we are thoroughly persuaded of the main results of modern criticism, and have rearranged the Bible in our own minds as the history of an orderly development culminating in Christ, the true Prince of mankind, and if this has fortified our own faith by a sense of historical veracity, we need not fear to speak plainly to the young; for we can hardly fail to convey to them the consciousness that the religious aim is paramount with us, and that we wish it to be so with them. When they can realize that, through the results of criticism,

The Bible and the Child

Christian piety and zeal are not slackened but increased, and that both the Old Testament history and Christ himself are made to stand out in clearer outline, the danger lest light and truth should in maturer life come to them as destructive and disintegrating powers will have passed away, and we may trust that the Bible will grow to them more real and more precious the more their knowledge and experience extend.

VI

The Bible as Literature

By the Rev. Washington Gladden, D.D.

VI

THE Bible is the book of religion, but it is also, by eminence, the book of literature. Well may we call it The Book; it is the prolific mother of books; since the invention of printing, the book-makers have been busy, a good share of their time, in producing Bibles, and books about the Bible.

The influence of our English Bible upon our language in keeping our speech simple and direct and unstilted is beyond all comprehension. Euphuistic dandyism and Johnsonese magniloquence have been slain by its homely eloquence; and not only have thirsty souls with joy drawn the water of life by its aid from the wells of salvation, but scholars and writers of books have drawn the freshness and grace of literary form from its pure well of English undefiled. It is scarcely an exaggeration to say that our greatest English writers have been the men who best knew their Bibles. John Bunyan read almost no other book, and he contrived to write a book of which, it is said, more copies have been printed than of any other English book except the Bible itself. Of men as far apart in their view of life as Byron and Ruskin, it could with equal truthfulness be said that their mastery of style is largely due to their perfect familiarity with the English Bible.

Complaints of the Bible as archaic and uncouth in its literary form have not, indeed, been wanting; and some of the most amusing books in the language are those which have undertaken to remedy this defect. A translation of the New Testament published

The Rev. Washington Gladden, D.D.

in New England in 1833, by an Episcopal clergyman, exhibits in its introduction the need of such a reconstructed Bible. "While various other works," says the translator, "and especially those of the most trivial attainment, are diligently adorned with a splendid and sweetly flowing diction, why should the mere uninteresting identity and paucity of language be so exclusively employed in rendering the Word of God? Why should the Christian Scriptures be divested even of decent ornament? Why should not an edition of the heavenly institutes be furnished for the reading-room, saloon, and toilet, as well as for the church, school, and nursery; for the literary and accomplished gentleman as well as for the plain and unlettered citizen?" This is what this fine writer essays to do, and a few samples of the way he does it may be instructive:

The Bible and the Child

When thou art beneficent, let not thy left hand know what thy right hand performs.

Contemplate the lilies of the field, how they advance.

At that time Jesus took occasion to say, I entirely concur with thee, O Father, Lord of heaven and earth.

Every plantation which my heavenly Father has not cultivated shall be extirpated.

Salt is salutary; but if the salt has become vapid, how can it be restored?

Be not surprised that I announced to thee, Ye must be reproduced.

For this the Father loves me, because I gave up my life to be afterwards resumed. No one divests me of it, but I personally resign it. I have authority to resign it, and I have authority to resume it.

There are numerous apartments in my Father's temple; if not, I would have informed you.

The Rev. Washington Gladden, D.D.

This will serve as an illustration of the kind of writing to which, for long periods, we might have been delivered, if it had not been for the better model, always in the hands of the common people, of the strong and simple Saxon of our English Bible.

Most true is the contention of Matthew Arnold that, although the Bible is the book of religion and the book of conduct, we cannot draw from it the religious and the moral truth of which it is the treasury unless we treat it as literature. Literature it is, beyond all controversy, and not science, nor philosophy, nor theology. Grievously do we abuse it when we take its phrases as theological formulas, and undertake to piece them together in what we call systematic theology. "To understand that the language of the Bible is fluid, passing, and literary, not rigid, fixed, and scientific, is the first step," says Arnold, "towards a right understanding of the Bible." It is a step which many theologians have never taken. If our Sunday-school teachers could get possession of this truth, a good foundation would be laid for a spiritual and vital theology. And then it would be well to go a little deeper and try to comprehend the fact that all language is an instrument which man has devised for himself — a tool which he has fashioned, and is all the while reshaping for his uses; that it is necessarily imperfect and fallible — never, at its best estate, an instrument of precision; and that the best we can hope for is an approximation to the perfect utterance in words of spiritual realities. That profound discussion of the nature of language in the introduction to Dr. Bushnell's *God in Christ* should be carefully studied by every one who tries to interpret

The Rev. Washington Gladden, D.D.

the Bible. In the application of what are called the exact sciences — as, for example, in engineering — it is often necessary to repeat measurements or tests a great many times, and take the average of results that greatly vary. And in the expression of highest truth by means of human language the same method must be employed. The thing has to be said over, many times, in many ways; one analogy after another must be suggested, one aspect after another considered, until, by comparison and combination of all these impressions, the mind reaches something like a complete apprehension. " If we find the writer," says Dr. Bushnell, " moving with a free motion, and tied to no one symbol, unless in some popular effort or for some single occasion; if we find him multiplying antagonisms, offering cross-views, and bringing us round the field to see how it looks from different points, then we are to presume that he has some truth in hand which it becomes us to know. We are to pass round accordingly with him, take up all his symbols, catch a view with him here and another there, use one thing to qualify another, and the other to shed light upon that, and by a process of this kind endeavour to comprehend his antagonisms, and settle into a complete view of his meaning." This is an excellent statement of what is meant when it is said that the Bible is literature, and must be studied as literature in order to be understood.

But while the spiritual and moral content of the Bible is always the main subject of our study the Bible is well worthy of our attention also on account of its literary form. It was the architectural splendour of his capital, no doubt, that the poet was thinking of

The Rev. Washington Gladden, D.D.

when he wrote: "Out of Zion, the perfection of beauty, God hath shined forth." If the beauty of architecture is one medium by which he may be manifested, the beauty of the moving epic, the rhythmic ode, the stately oration, the sparkling epigram, is another and a far more perfect medium. The literary beauty of the Scriptures is not an accident; beauty is an essential element of all divine revelation, and as such deserves our most reverent study.

What Professor Moulton describes as "literary morphology" is a matter of interest, and the attempt which he has made, in his recent volume entitled *The Literary Study of the Bible* to give us some account of the leading forms of literature preserved for us in the Scriptures — to show us "how to distinguish one literary composition from another, to say exactly where each begins and ends; to recognize epic, lyric, and other forms as they appear in their Biblical dress, as well as to distinguish literary forms special to the sacred writers," is one to which the attention of all students of the English Bible may well be called. But more important than these technical distinctions is the recognition of the grace and loveliness with which the language of the Bible is often clothed. The power to discern this beauty needs to be cultivated. "Consider the lilies," said the Master. The word seems to mean that we are to sit down among them and study them, to pore over their loveliness until it enters into our souls and takes possession. I know not why so many of the fair flowers of speech are strewn upon the pages of the Book of books, unless it be that their beauty is meant to appeal to our thought and to give us a high and pure pleasure. Consider

The Rev. Washington Gladden, D.D.

these blossoms also. This is an integral part of the Gospel of God — the revelation of beauty. He saves from that which is low and base by offering us pleasure in that which is high and pure. " Let each one of us," says the Apostle, "*please* his neighbour for that which is good, unto edifying." It is thus that we become the children of our Father in heaven. And the Book which above all others reveals Him, offers to our minds abundant pleasure in the graces of beautiful speech.

It may be supposed that such a message as the Bible contains could have been delivered to men in language as tame and unimaginative as that of the Westminster Confession or the Thirty-nine Articles — that God's Bible might have contained no poetry, no music, no kindling eloquence. But such a supposition could not long be entertained by a thoroughly sane mind. The

The Bible and the Child

truth about God's love for man and man's life in God cannot be told in cold, logical formularies; the words into which it is poured will glow and burn; the sentences which are charged with it fall into rhythmic beat and reverberation. The hope and joy and glory of it are the best of it, and these cannot be put into logical propositions. The creeds are not the Gospel, any more than the skeleton is the man. The Gospel is not the Gospel when it is separated from the forms of beauty with which it came forth from the heart of God.

The question how the children who are studying the Bible can be made to discern and enjoy this beauty is one to which I am not inclined to propose any definite solution. The main thing is that those who teach the book shall themselves be filled with a sense of its beauty; out of the abundance of the

The Rev. Washington Gladden, D.D.

heart the mouth will speak. It would be well for all teachers to study Mr. Moulton's book; but it would not be well for them to burden the minds of their pupils with the technical distinctions of literary form.

To read the Bible with the pupils — if one can read well — selecting those narratives which are most dramatic and those poems which are most beautiful, is the best way of conveying to their minds the sense of its beauty. We read so much by chapters, and study so much by scraps and sentences, that the sense of literary unities is scarcely awakened at all. To read through, at one sitting, or continuously, with judicious omissions, the story of Abraham, or the story of Joseph, or the story of Elijah, or the story of David, or the story of Ruth — not stopping to make many expository comments, and only pointing out the defective ethical standards which the stories often imply, when they are judged by Christ's perfect rule—would be a most valuable exercise in a Sunday-school class. The narratives can be trusted to make their own impression, and it would be difficult to find language more picturesque or attractive than that in which the Bible clothes them. A little maid of seven, after listening with interest to the reading of Bible stories paraphrased for children, said, with a sigh, "Yes, that is good; but I like the real Bible better."

The reading of the lyrical portions of the Bible with young people a little more mature might also be profitable. Such magnificent odes as the Song of Moses and Miriam, the Song of Deborah, the Song of David, should be read through with the pupils, and not marred or belittled by a word of passing comment. To return, after the reading, and

The Rev. Washington Gladden, D.D.

call attention to the music of the phrases, the march of the rhetoric, and the splendour of the imagery, would be judicious. But the principal qualification of the teacher is the ability to feel, and to express in his own reading, the lyrical beauty of the poetry. Many of the Psalms and the Prophecies, not a few of the discourses of our Lord, and notable passages in the Epistles and in the Apocalypse, can be treated in the same way. The arrangement of these poetical materials which Mr. Moulton has given us, in strophe and antistrophe, and in what he calls lower and higher parallelisms, while sometimes fanciful, is, on the whole, very helpful to the appreciation of the poetry, and would greatly assist the teacher who sought, by such a method, to convey to his pupils the beauty of the forms in which the saving truth of the Bible is expressed.

VII

The Higher Criticism and the Teaching of the Young

By the Rev. Frank C. Porter, Ph.D.
Professor in Yale Divinity School

VII

THE question how far the results of the historical criticism of the Bible should be used in the instruction of children is, for those who accept these results, in part a question of truth, and in part of expediency; but it is also in part a question of profit, and in this aspect I wish to consider it. The historical criticism of the Bible means the use of its books as historical sources; and this means that the student does not value the book simply as a book, but is looking for something that lies behind the book. The question, not indeed of the right — let this be taken for granted — but of the worth of criticism resolves itself, therefore, into the question, Which is of greater value, the book as a book, or the historical facts and persons behind the book? Does critical study take us from the less to the greater, or from the greater to the less? If it leads to the less, we need not trouble children and the world at large with it; if to the greater, we must offer the new treasure to all. We cannot accept the historian's natural answer to the question, for his common fault is an over-valuation of his work. To be sure, the movement from fiction to fact is a movement up, but the movement from *truth* to fact is a movement down. It does not much matter whence Shakespeare got his stories, and how much fact, how much fiction, they contain; and the critic, who must ask these questions, should not suppose that he is doing the greater thing in answering them. Scholars will analyze and excavate in the effort to go back of Homer, and decide

The Rev. Frank C. Porter, Ph.D.

whether he was one or many, and what was fact, what fiction, about Troy and its fall. But the story is worth more than the fact behind it. It is the universal and the eternal in Shakespeare and Homer, not the local and temporal, that we wish the child to gain and to love. On the other hand, there are great events in human history whose significance far surpasses that of their records, so that to make our way through records to the facts is to go from the less to the greater.

Is the virtue of the Bible, then, like that of Homer and Shakespeare in that it lies in the books as books, or is the virtue in the facts behind the books? It is in neither alone, but in both in very different degrees; and upon the recognition of this fact the solution of our problem turns. It is worth while to let children accompany the historian as fast and as far as they can, when the events and personalities of which a book tells are more profitable than the book itself for teaching, for reproof, for correction, for instruction in righteousness. But the discovery that every book in the Bible has interest and value as a historical source should not lead us to suppose that this is the chief interest and value of all alike. The historical interest is, indeed, now somewhat domineering. It threatens to deprive us of the free and happy appreciation of story as story, of poetry as poetry, in its anxiety to know facts. In an age of science we must fight on every hand for our æsthetic enjoyment, our spiritual appreciation of things as they are, because we are so possessed by the passion to get back to things as they were, and as they came to be.

There is in the Bible much story and

The Rev. Frank C. Porter, Ph.D.

poetry which is of value for the spirit that is in it more than for the facts that are behind it. The Hebrew mind expressed its religious sentiments and ideals by preference in imagery and narrative. The Gospels teach us how effective the parable may be as the language of religion. And the parable, in a large sense, is much more extensively used in the Bible than our prosaic minds readily perceive. There will be, it is true, much diversity of opinion regarding the question where the story, where the fact, is of greater religious value. Religion may demand the actual where art would be content with the ideal. But the case is often clear. It is of far more use for us to know the mind of the writer of Job than the facts or traditions with which he deals. It is in the book that these get their value. Of other poetical books of the Old Testament the same is true; of Proverbs, of Ecclesiastes, and of the Psalms. Historical questions in the case of these books are peculiarly hard, for the very reason that their connection with history is so slight. But books in the historical form, also, may be more important as books than as histories. This is especially true when they are not the work of individuals, but are formed in a national tradition and take into themselves the spirit of a people's life. The stories of the beginnings of Israel's history are such products of the Israelitish genius. This is the source of their perennial charm. These products of the youthful spirit of Israel are, indeed, in our Bible, mixed with the work of a later age and a different spirit. One must read the prophetic apart from the priestly narratives if he would feel the breath of the dawn of the nation's life. For this distinction we are

The Rev. Frank C. Porter, Ph.D.

dependent upon the historical critic. Let us by all means give to children the advantage of this distinction in their reading of the Bible, and let us explain it to them when they ask for the explanation or need it. But let not the critic spoil for us, young or old, the charm of these stories because he does not know how much in them is history and how much legend. Let children read them as they are, but see that they seize upon their spirit, so that if questions of fact afterward arise they may feel that their treasure in the story does not depend upon the answer.

But, on the other hand, the Bible records events that are in themselves of the greatest religious significance, great as evidences of the hand of God in human history, great as causes of progress and achievement in the religious life of humanity. Such events were the exodus from Egypt, the establishment of the kingdom of Israel, its division, the fall of Samaria, the captivity and the return of Judah. In and through these events great movements of life and thought were initiated in which we are still borne onward — movements significant not only in their ideal contents, but in their historical actuality. Whatever the charm of the record, the facts are more impressive, and we are more concerned to know the facts as they were than to keep the records as they are. Here historical science, in passing through the records to the facts, contributes to a larger and truer faith in God. When criticism pushes aside the overgrowth and brings to light some hidden flower of rare beauty, its work is of far greater value to the spirit of man than when it proceeds to pull the flower to pieces. Children should be shown the flower, for

The Rev. Frank C. Porter, Ph.D.

they cannot find it by themselves; but to the deeper knowledge of it loving contemplation is a better way than analysis.

In the events just mentioned certain actors appear — the prophets — in regard to whom one hesitates to say whether they disclosed the significance of the events, or gave the events their significance; whether the events or these personalities were the more immediate work of God. They were certainly the supreme flower of Israel's religious life, and it is one of the chief contributions of historical science to religious faith that it has given us a closer view of these men. Yet, just here where the religious value of historical methods is most evident, it is perhaps hardest to know how to make use of them for immature minds.

Behind the Book of Isaiah, for example, stands the prophet Isaiah, who is greater than the book. Not only for history, but for religion, we value the book chiefly as a means of acquainting us with one of the greatest of the men of faith; and we are ready to do with the book whatever will help us to reach the man. But between us and Isaiah stands the copyist, and back of him the scribe. The Revisers in their preface let us know what hard work the copyists have made us, and how far textual criticism is from having undone all their errors in the Old Testament. But the scribes have left us a still harder task. Our Book of Isaiah is their work, not his. They were wrong in ascribing all this material to him. Not only chapters 40–66, but parts of chapters 1–39, cannot be from Isaiah, nor from Isaiah's age. If we would know him, we must set these parts aside — not that they are of less value for history or for religion than the rest, but

The Rev. Frank C. Porter, Ph.D.

that they are not of value in the search for Isaiah. Further, the events with reference to which Isaiah spoke must be known, the background of his time, and even what came before and after, the sources and effects of his life, if we would know him. And, finally, after all this preparation, there is needed that sympathetic inward response of soul to soul, by which alone one man knows another. So that our knowledge of Isaiah is conditioned on the one side by much difficult scientific research, and on the other side by our spiritual capacity, our inner relationship to him.

Of these two conditions of the right understanding and good use of a book of Scripture, either one may be overestimated. If the condition of scholarship is emphasized, we may be forced to some such position as this. Children and untrained persons cannot follow the hard path just described, even if they have a guide; while the uncritical reading of the book will surely lead them astray from the true path. It is, therefore, better that they should not read the book at all, but should receive its treasures at second hand. Let the historical expert, through a highly special kind of skilled labour, make his way into the presence of the great personalities of Biblical history, and get from the vision and contact fresh moral and religious impulses which shall become a part of his own personal life. Then let him impart this possession to others, not as he gained it, but directly, in the language of to-day, and by the heightened power of his own personality. This result has actually been reached of late by a young German critic. But such intervention of the scholar between the Christian and his

The Rev. Frank C. Porter, Ph.D.

Bible is as intolerable as the Roman Catholic intervention of the priest. The learned have, as a matter of experience, no such advantage over the unlearned in gaining from the Scriptures eternal life. Children and childlike men are not less fitted than others to apprehend and appropriate the Christian religion, but, according to the testimony of its founder, they are better fitted than the wise.

This brings us to the other condition for the right use of the Bible. If childlike humility and trust alone are needed, the question may arise whether historical science is at all worth while, whether it does not rather lead one aside from the best uses of the book. This, too, has been recently maintained in Germany.[1] It has been asserted that what the Bible, as it is, offers to

[1] By Professor Kähler, of Halle.

the simple and true-hearted reader is everywhere of far greater value than anything that historical science, with all its uncertainties, can discover behind the book; and that the search for the less is a positive hindrance to the finding of the greater.

I believe that in both of these extreme views the difficulties of the historical process are exaggerated. To be sure, path-breakers in the historical field must be rarely equipped, but less gifted minds can pursue the path when it has once been made, and can recognize the truth of conclusions which they could never have reached alone. The main conclusions of the critical school rest, not on matters of philological or archæological detail, but upon considerations which appeal to the common reason of men; and in proportion to their importance and security are their grounds broad and general and capable

The Rev. Frank C. Porter, Ph.D.

of popularization. The common mind is more and more accessible to scientific truths in their large outlines, and its need is measured by its capacity.

On the other hand, it is true that the scientific study of the Bible is only preparatory, even when the preparation is quite essential, to that inward appreciation, that sympathetic insight, that response of feeling and will, which is a matter of character, not of learning. In the reading of no other book does this factor play so large a part. One will find in the Bible what he has the moral and spiritual capacity to find. Yet the preparation is essential. Historical criticism is only the effort to answer the characteristic intellectual questions of our age. We cannot and would not silence the questions. To children they will be even more natural and inevitable than they are to us, and children

The Bible and the Child

have a right to the best answer we can give. It is not in point to say that the past found the spiritual treasure of the Bible without asking such questions. For our age they are vital questions, and they must have our attention, whether we are glad or sorry to give it, if the book is to keep its old power and gain new power over the heart and will of men.

I would have the child study the Book of Isaiah in such a way as to find the man, believing that the sight of the man will call forth admiration and love, and will be a greater power in the child's life, making for faith and righteousness, than the book as it is could be.

The heart of the Bible is the Gospels, and here our problem centres. Here are books of matchless beauty and power, yet behind them stands a person who is greater than the books. Historical students cannot but try

The Rev. Frank C. Porter, Ph.D.

to go back of the books to the person. By a comparison of the Gospels with each other, they will look for the actual deeds and words of Jesus; by a comparison of these with each other they will search for his ruling thoughts and purposes; by a study of his race and age they will seek for the influences that determined the outward course of his life and the direction and form of his teaching, that they may distinguish the new from the old, the inward from the outward, the spirit from the form. Yet, after all their efforts to unveil behind the Gospels the features of Christ, what they see will depend upon what they are, the sight of Christ being still, as it was when he was on earth, the testing and the making of character. And yet the historical work is a help. The clearer our outward vision of Jesus, the easier is the inward approach to him, for it is oftener true that intellectual difficulties put obstacles in the way of the impulse of the heart toward Christ, than that the intellectual view satisfies the mind and stills the heart's impulse.

Children, then, should not be deprived of the help that criticism can give in the study of the Christ of the Gospels. Indeed, the teacher who reads the Gospels in their relations to one another, and who puts the lifework of Jesus in its historical setting, will not be able to teach the youngest person without using, directly or indirectly, the light derived from these studies. At an early age the life and words of Jesus should be studied by the comparison of parallel accounts in the different Gospels. The study of the Gospels in their individuality should come afterwards. The first search is for Christ himself. Let the peculiarities of each Gospel be left aside

The Rev. Frank C. Porter, Ph.D.

at first, and let attention be given to the material common to two or more Gospels. The use of Stevens and Burton's *Harmony of the Gospels for Historical Study* or of Waddy's *Harmony of the Four Gospels*[1] in Sunday-schools is, I believe, advisable. The advantages of such comparative study of the Gospels are many. Most obviously it brings us nearer to the very words and deeds of Jesus. It suggests the answer to many questions that perplex the child's mind as well as the man's. It imparts the right view of Scripture as a whole, freeing the child at the outset from that bondage to the letter from which many have broken away only to lose, with the letter, the spiritual treasure which is nowhere else to be found.

[1] The Revised Version is used in both; the former gives important parallels in foot-notes which do not fall into a harmonistic scheme; the latter gives aid to the comparison of the text in detail.

Further, the child should be taught the outward and inward conditions of the life of Christ. He could early read such a book as Morrison's *Jews under Roman Rule* with interest. And the habit of viewing the life of Jesus in its historical connections could easily be formed. By such a view one's sense of the uniqueness of Christ is heightened, and, on the other hand, the distinction between the form and the spirit, between the temporal and the eternal, in the earthly life of Jesus is more readily perceived.

These two things the child should learn — to find Christ in the Gospels, and to find the Eternal in Christ. When he has done this, he has solved in essence the problem of his religious life, and he has solved also in principle the lesser problem of the Bible and its use.

The vision of the person of Christ is the

The Rev. Frank C. Porter, Ph.D.

end of all Biblical study, and by its relation to the end all else is to be understood; the vision of Christ within, but behind and above the Gospels: within, so that he may be found by one who reads the Gospels as they are with a childlike heart; but behind, so that if the veil of writing be somewhat pushed apart, his form will be more fully disclosed; and yet again above, so that when we see him and hear him as he was, we still need to translate his words and deeds out of the language of a certain age and race into the universal language of the spirit, that we may hear him speaking not to others but to us.

It is the great service of the historical criticism of the Bible, that of the Old Testament as well as that of the New, that it gives help, which is to the modern mind indispensable, to the more direct vision and deeper apprehension of Christ. One to whom it renders this service will not withhold it from children, and will not do harm by its misuse.

VIII

The Bible as Rearranged by Modern Criticism

By the Rev. Lyman Abbott, D.D.

VIII

I IMAGINE before me a class of intelligent boys and girls from twelve years of age and upwards. They have studied something of ancient history, and know something of the growth of nations. To this class of boys and girls I address myself in this article, endeavouring to tell them, as far as it is possible so to do within the compass of so brief an article, what the modern scholar thinks about the construction and growth of the Old Testament.[1]

More than three thousand years ago, before Virgil or Horace had written their

[1] Of course all scholars are not agreed. The views here embodied may be defined, perhaps, as those of the more conservative of the modern school.

poems, or Cicero or Demosthenes had delivered their orations; before Cæsar had crossed the Rubicon, or Alexander had ridden Bucephalus, or the Greeks had met the Persians at the battle of Marathon; yes! before Homer had sung the songs which bear his name, or Trojan and Greek had met in battle about the walls of Troy; when everywhere government was despotism, and religion was superstition — there dwelt, in a most horrible form of slavery, a singular people, in a province of Egypt. By a series of remarkable deliverances they were set free from bondage, and, crossing a northern arm of the Red Sea and traversing the wilderness of Arabia, encamped in a great plain at the foot of one of the majestic and awful mountains in the south of the Arabian Peninsula. Here their great leader and prophet gave them their constitution. It was at once

The Rev. Lyman Abbott, D.D.

political and religious. It was very simple and yet it was very radical. The Egyptians, from whose land this people had come forth, worshipped a great multitude of gods. Their learned men, indeed, said to one another that there really is but one God, and that the deities whom the people worshipped were but manifestations of him, if they were not merely imaginations of the people. This belief, however, they kept to themselves. Moses, by his declarations, made it the common faith of the children of Israel. "Hear, O Israel," he said; "Jehovah your God is one God." He told them further that this God was a righteous God; that He demanded righteousness of His children, and that He demanded nothing else. This seems very simple to us now, but it was very strange and very radical doctrine in the world then. Founded on this simple prin-

The Bible and the Child

ciple, he gave this people their religious and political constitution. It is known in Hebrew history as the Book of the Covenant, and is contained in the 20th, 21st, 22d, and 23d chapters of the Book of Exodus.[1] This, with the possible exception of a few odes and songs, is probably the most ancient writing in the Bible; it is certainly its most ancient teaching. It contains the famous Ten Commandments; which declare that the people should reverence God, honour their parents, respect each other's rights of person, the family, property, and reputation. These simple principles it elaborates and applies with a number of specific illustrations. It contains no directions to perform sacrifices, no instruction respecting ritualism, and makes no provision for a priesthood.

[1] By some believed to begin with xx. 23, and not to include the Ten Commandments.

The Rev. Lyman Abbott, D.D.

The Israelites, after spending a number of years in the wilderness, entered upon a campaign against the inhabitants of Canaan and took possession of their land. The story of this campaign is written in the Book of Joshua. There followed a period of nearly three centuries, which we may describe as colonial days, the story of which is contained in the Book of Judges and the first part of the Book of Samuel. During this time there was no true capital, indeed no true nation. There were a variety of separate provinces, having almost as little common life as the American colonies before the formation of the Constitution of the United States. In war these colonies united; in peace they separated from each other again. At length, weary of perpetual jealousy and strife, and desirous of emulating the example of other nations about them, they established a monarchy, and David came as the second king to the throne. In many respects David resembles King Alfred the Great of England. He had a profoundly religious nature, and it found expression in odes and psalms so striking, if not so numerous, that they have given his name to the Hebrew hymn-book. He was a great warrior, and in his early life the leader of an irresponsible band of outlaws, though always an intense patriot. He had a profoundly religious spirit, and a capacity for statesmanship and a power of organization very remarkable. Under his forty years of administration the colonies were welded into one measurably harmonious nation. How this nation grew in wealth and splendour, but not in real prosperity, under Solomon, the foolish wise king; how it split in sunder under his son; how its divided life was sub-

The Rev. Lyman Abbott, D.D.

sequently carried on in two separate historical currents, as the life of Israel and the life of Judah; how the land became the battleground of contending nations — Egypt on the south, Assyria, Persia, Babylon, and Chaldea on the east; how at last the Israelites were carried away captive, dispersed, and have disappeared from human history; how a little later the Jews, or inhabitants of Judæa, were also carried away captive, but retained their religious faith and their distinctive characteristics in the land of their captivity, is told in the Books of Kings and Chronicles. And how of the latter there returned, after seventy years of exile, a number of immigrants to rebuild Jerusalem and take up again the story of national life, the mere remnant of a nation, and under adverse circumstances, is told in the Books of Ezra and Nehemiah.

The Bible and the Child

During the progress of this history there were two religious forces at work among this people, very much as during later history in Europe. These two forces may be characterized as the ecclesiastical and the non-ecclesiastical, the priestly and the prophetic. In European history the priestly tendency was largely represented by the Roman Catholic Church, the prophetic by the Reformed or Protestant Churches; in England the priestly by the High Church party in the Established Church, the prophetic by the Puritan and Wesleyan movements; in New England the priestly or ecclesiastical by the Puritan established church, and the prophetical or non-ecclesiastical by the Baptists, the Quakers, and the Independents. But in every church and in every community both elements are more or less to be seen — sometimes sharply separated, sometimes closely commingled.

The Rev. Lyman Abbott, D.D.

During the period of Jewish history both these elements grew up together. Moses had probably at the close of his life delivered a farewell address analogous in some respects to the famous farewell address of Washington. Traditions of this address had been preserved, possibly in documents, more probably in oral reports. In that age of the world oral tradition was far more enduring and trustworthy than it is in our time, when we trust to written and printed records in place of verbal memory. In one of the great reformations which occurred in Jewish history an unknown prophet, desirous to revive the moral law and re-establish its sanctity, gathered together these traditions and recast them in a book which he called The Second Giving of the Law. It was dramatically represented as being Moses' farewell address, though the author did not intend to deceive, nor, in fact, did deceive, the people of the age in which the book appeared. This is the Book of Deuteronomy, supposed to have been written about eight hundred years after the death of Moses. It has very little to say about church observances and a great deal to say about practical righteousness. It embodies the prophetic or non-ecclesiastical religious teaching which had descended from Moses and had been kept alive in the nation by his successors.

Meanwhile, a very different religious life had been developed in this nation — the priestly or ecclesiastical. From a very early period in human history, so remote that scholars do not know when the practice began, it has been the custom among pagan people to express their religious sentiments, whether of gratitude for the goodness of the gods, of penitence for sin against the gods,

The Rev. Lyman Abbott, D.D.

of desire for the forgiveness of the gods, or of consecration to the service of the gods, by sacrifices. Sometimes these have been of great magnitude, hundreds of cattle being slain at once. Not infrequently human sacrifices have been offered to appease the wrath or win the favour of supposed deities. The Jewish ecclesiastical law accepted this custom and embodied it in the Jewish ritual, but it made two radical changes : it declared that the value of the sacrifice depended, not on the value of the article sacrificed, but on the spirit of the person offering it; and it laid stress upon the truth that there was no legal obligation to offer such services, that to be of any value they must be the free-will offering of the worshipper, and must express his real and sincere sentiment. " He shall offer it of his own voluntary will at the door of the tabernacle of the congregation before

The Bible and the Child

the Lord," was the fundamental provision of the ecclesiastical code. But as time went on, these sacrifices, which at first were very simple, grew more and more elaborate. A temple was constructed where they were to be offered. Probably at first custom, eventually law, forbade offering them anywhere else. At first a father might offer for his family, or a king for his people, but later the priesthood took the whole control of the sacrificial system, and no offerings were counted legitimate except those which passed through the hands of the priesthood. This code, which was nearly a thousand years in growing up, was finally embodied in a series of written regulations, most of which were contained in the Book of Leviticus, but some also in Exodus and some in Numbers. This code, so strangely different from the simple moral law of the Book of the

The Rev. Lyman Abbott, D.D.

Covenant and the second giving of the law — the Book of Deuteronomy — embodies the priestly or ecclesiastical life of the nation as it had grown up in and around the Temple in Jerusalem during a thousand years.

While this growth was taking place in the prophetic and in the ecclesiastical life of the kingdom, there was also growing up among the Jews a literature. The most notable portion of this literature consisted of sermons or addresses delivered by men who were at once preachers, reformers, and statesmen. They fulfilled this threefold function much as John Calvin did in Geneva, as Knox did in Scotland, and as the Puritan preachers did in New England. The preacher in a theocracy is the public counsellor both of the officers and of the people. These sermons or addresses — sometimes they were songs sung to the accompaniment of a harp, and often were poetic in their form — were, in the course of time, collected under the names of the principal preachers. The book, however, not infrequently bore the name of one preacher, while it contained utterances of several. This is especially the case with the Book of Isaiah and with that of Zechariah. In such a case the principal author gave his name to the entire collection. Many of these prophecies are unintelligible, or almost unintelligible, to the reader of our ordinary English Bible, because he does not know the historical conditions under which they were uttered. His state of mind in respect to them is like that of one who should read Daniel Webster's reply to Hayne without knowing that there was a United States of America and a threatened movement to nullify the National laws, if not to secede from the Nation.

The Rev. Lyman Abbott, D.D.

The hymns of the Jewish nation which grew up through the long period of its history from the time of David, if not from the time of Moses, down almost to the time of Christ, were gathered together, as in our day hymns in common use are gathered together in hymn-books. This Hebrew hymn-book is known as the Book of Psalms. I have no doubt that David contributed some of the most beautiful of these Psalms to the collection, though this is doubted by some scholars. But it is quite certain that a majority of them were written at a much later date, and many of them while the Jews were captives in Babylon, or after their return to the Holy Land. The other books of the Old Testament would be classified in ordinary literature, probably, as belles-lettres. How far those which are historical in their form have a historical basis of truth we cannot now judge. They are to be regarded, however, as literature, not as history. Such is the Book of Ruth — a beautiful idyl of the colonial days, illustrating the sincerity and simplicity of woman's love; the Book of Esther — a dramatic story, illustrating woman's courage and glowing with splendid patriotism; the Book of Job, which has been well called an "epic of the inner life," and which some eminent critics have characterized as the noblest poem in literature; the Book of Ecclesiastes — in appearance a monologue, but in reality a dialogue, in which "The Two Voices" in man, as Tennyson calls them, the voice of cynicism and that of spiritual hope, struggle for victory; and the Song of Solomon — a love drama in which a maiden resists all the flatteries and blandishments of the king who would make her queen of his harem, and remains faithful to

The Rev. Lyman Abbott, D.D.

her peasant lover, to whom at last she returns in purity and happiness. To these must be added the Book of Proverbs, a collection of the wise sayings and apophthegms which grew up in the nation during the thousand years of its history, and which took the name of Solomon because of his historic reputation for worldly wisdom. Had it been written by one man, we might have described him as the Benjamin Franklin of his age and community. Finally, we must add, last of all, though the date of its composition is uncertain, the Book of Genesis; that is, the Book of Origins. This was written late in Hebrew history, as a kind of introduction to the historical books. In it the author takes the legends of a pre-historic time as he finds them floating in tradition of his own and other nations, and rewrites them, writing God and Divine truth into them, somewhat

The Bible and the Child

as Tennyson took the Arthurian legends and rewrote them in *The Idylls of the King*, sometimes interpreting moral beauty which he discovered in them, sometimes imparting to them moral beauty which they did not before possess.

This is the Old Testament. It is a collection of Hebrew literature; it includes law, history, hymnody, drama, fiction, poetry, and moral and religious teaching; perhaps I might say sermons. Its earliest important writing is the Book of the Covenant; its latest, probably some of the Psalms. Its Book of Deuteronomy is an elaboration and amplification of the political and religious instruction of the founder of the commonwealth. Its Book of Leviticus is an elaboration of the liturgical code which grew up during eight hundred years or more of church life. Its literature is as various and

The Rev. Lyman Abbott, D.D.

as splendid as can be found in that of any other nation in an equal length of time, though not as voluminous. And the whole collection is pervaded by the great, simple, inspiring religious ideas that there is one God, that He is a righteous God, that He demands righteousness of His children, and that if they desire righteousness He will forgive their sins and help them to become worthy to be called His children. This message to Israel by its prophets, this message of Israel to the world, this revelation of God and His righteousness and His redeeming love, constitute the value of a book which has not only no peer, but nothing parallel or analogous to it in this respect in the literature of the world, and make it a fitting preparation for the New Testament, in which this revelation of God reaches its climax in the life of Jesus Christ.